T-Bot and Peabody

Explore The Zoo

By Jonathan D. Fluck

Copyright © 2011 by Jonathan D. Fluck

All rights reserved. This book or any portion thereof
may not be reproduced or used in any manner whatsoever
without the express written permission of the publisher
except for the use of brief quotations in a book review.

Peabody character is based upon Macouno's "Petunia".

Printed in the United States of America

First Printing, 2011

ISBN-13: 978-1463696122

ISBN-10: 1463696124

Edited by Karen Fluck

Website: www.TBotAndPeabody.com

*Ethan and Ephraim, may your curiosity never be satisfied and your friendship never ending.
Karen, thank you for inspiring and encouraging me.*

www.TBotAndPeabody.com

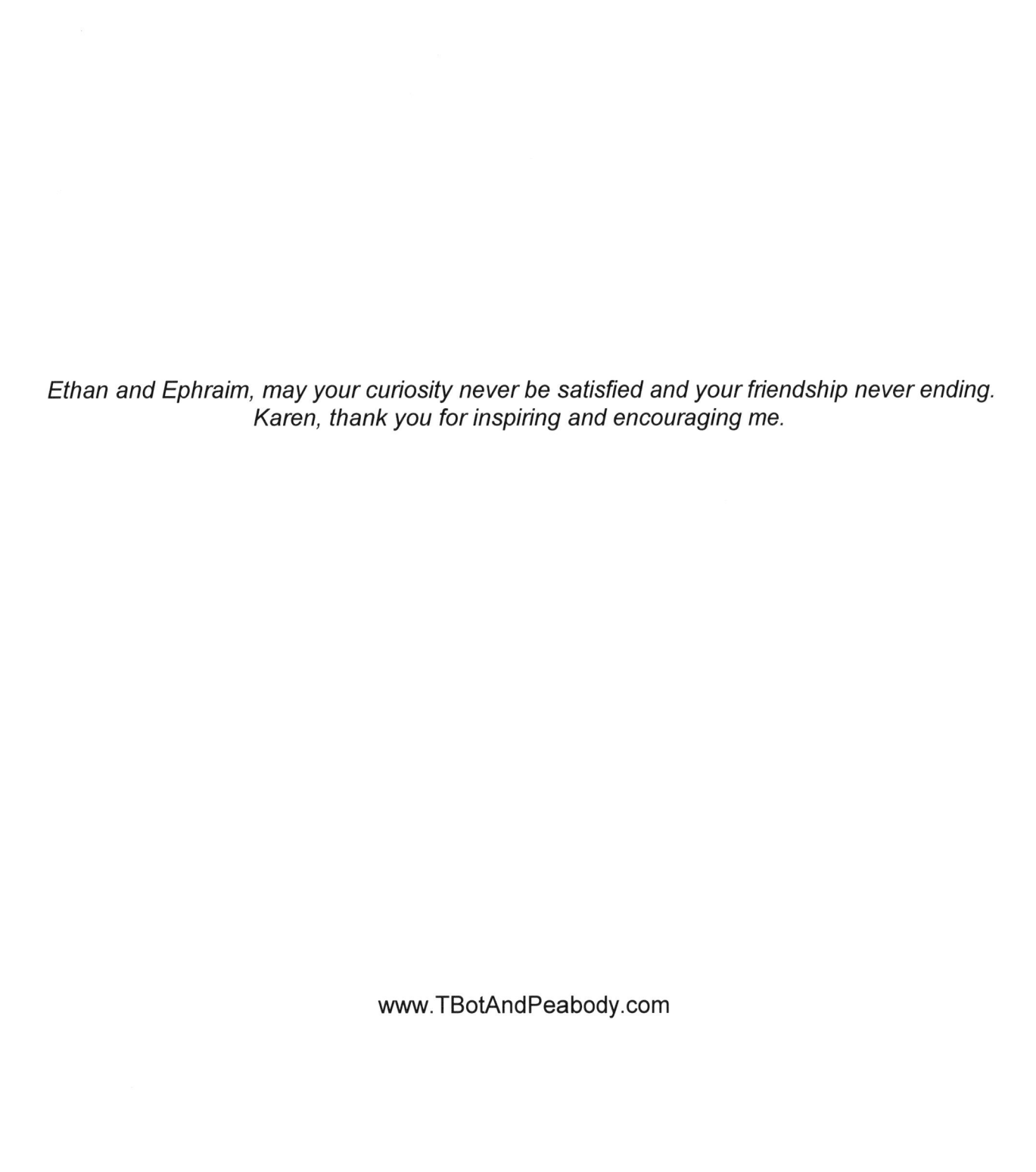

HELLO

My Name is...
Peabody

HELLO

My Name is...
T-Bot

T-Bot and Peabody are two robot brothers. They like to explore together and learn new things. Today they are exploring the zoo.

The zoo is filled with animals from all around the world. Some animals are big like the giraffe and others are small like the monkey.

While exploring the zoo the two brothers see some rhinoceroses. The rhino is an herbivore. He likes to eat leafy plants, branches, and fruit. An adult black rhino can weigh as much as a car!

Peabody noticed that there was a camel in the Rhino's pen and was afraid that the camel was lost. T-Bot explained that sometimes different animals live together at the zoo. This makes the zoo feel more like their home in the wild. It's called environmental enrichment.

Environmental enrichment makes the animals happier by providing them with games to play, puzzles to solve, and tools to use.

T-Bot's computer heard him talking about environmental enrichment and told them other ways animal's lives are enriched at the zoo.

Capuchin Monkey

1. His home is in South Amercia.

2. He spends most of his time in the trees.

3. His favorite foods are nuts and insects.

Peabody was getting excited watching the animals and started to jump around and waving his arms. T-Bot's computer thought he was a monkey and started telling them all about the capuchin monkey.

What they learned was so interesting they decided to go visit the capuchin monkey. The monkey was hard to see because he was climbing high in the trees.

While T-Bot was studying facts about the capuchin monkey, Peabody saw an amazing animal peeking his head over the trees. It was a very tall giraffe. Did you know that the giraffe can be as tall as a 2 story house? It looks like these two giraffes are sharing a secret. What do you think they are saying?

Giraffe

1. His favorite meal is thorny leaves of the Acacia tree.

2. His tongue can be up to 21 inches long.

3. The giraffe is the tallest mammal and lives in Africa.

T-Bot was in the middle of teaching Peabody all about giraffes when all of the sudden they felt the ground shake and heard a loud trumpeting noise. It was the largest land animal in the world walking around. That's right, it was an elephant! The two brothers had to go meet him.

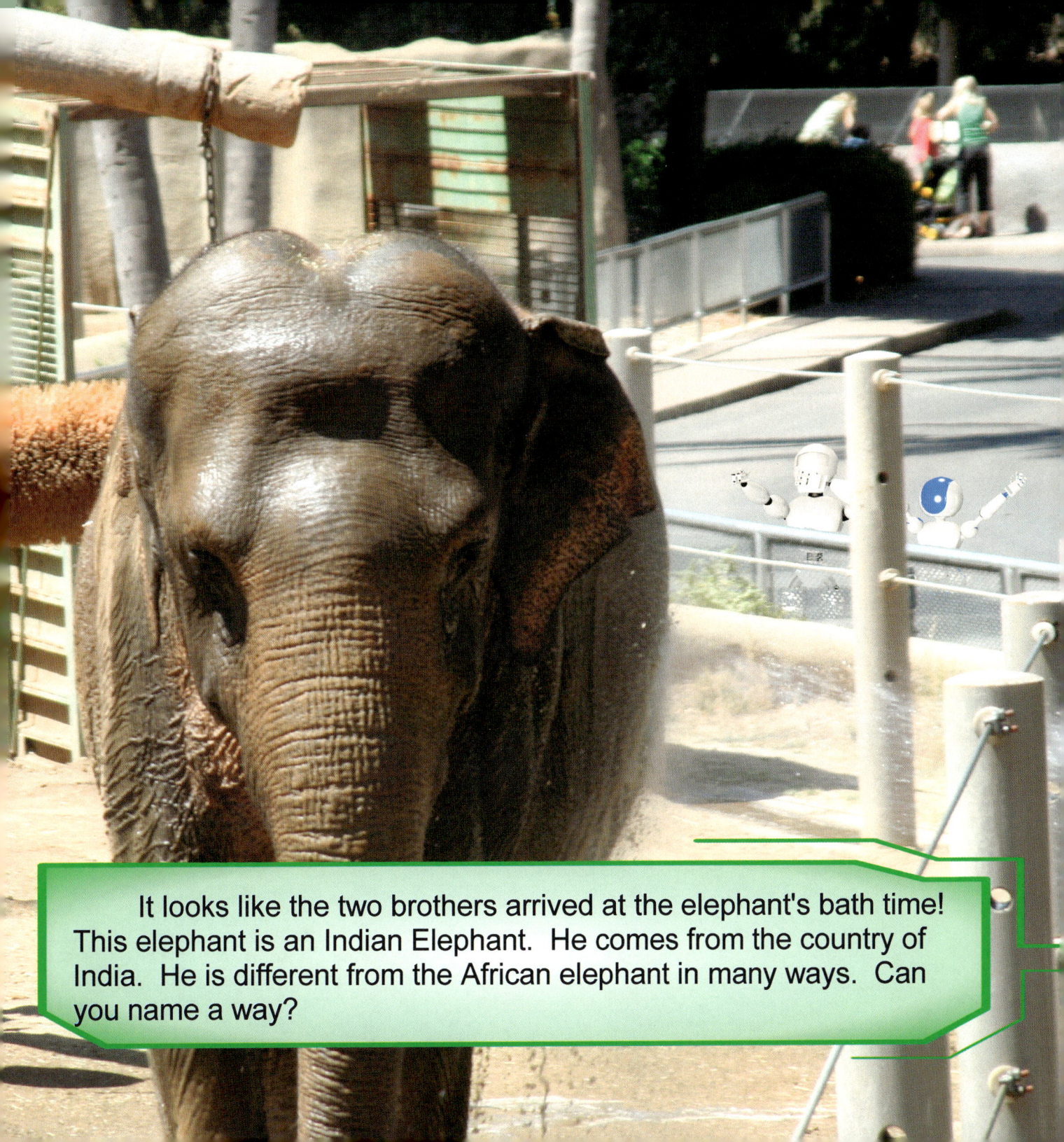

It looks like the two brothers arrived at the elephant's bath time! This elephant is an Indian Elephant. He comes from the country of India. He is different from the African elephant in many ways. Can you name a way?

African Elephant

- 8 - 14 feet tall
- Big Ears
- 2 finger like projections on trunk
- 4 Toenails
- Grazes for plants in the grasslands
- Lives in Africa

Asian Elephant

- 2 Round Bumps
- Small Ears
- Usually browse for food in the forest
- 5 Toenails
- 1 finger like projection on trunk
- 7 - 12 feet tall
- Lives in India

African Elephant

1. Adult females and their young travel in a herd.

2. Elephants use their tusks to dig up roots.

3. Elephants can eat up to 300 pounds of food a day.

Our two robot brothers had an exciting time at the zoo and learned many new things. Most of all they had fun playing with all their new friends. T-Bot and Peabody will be best friends forever.

Animal Facts

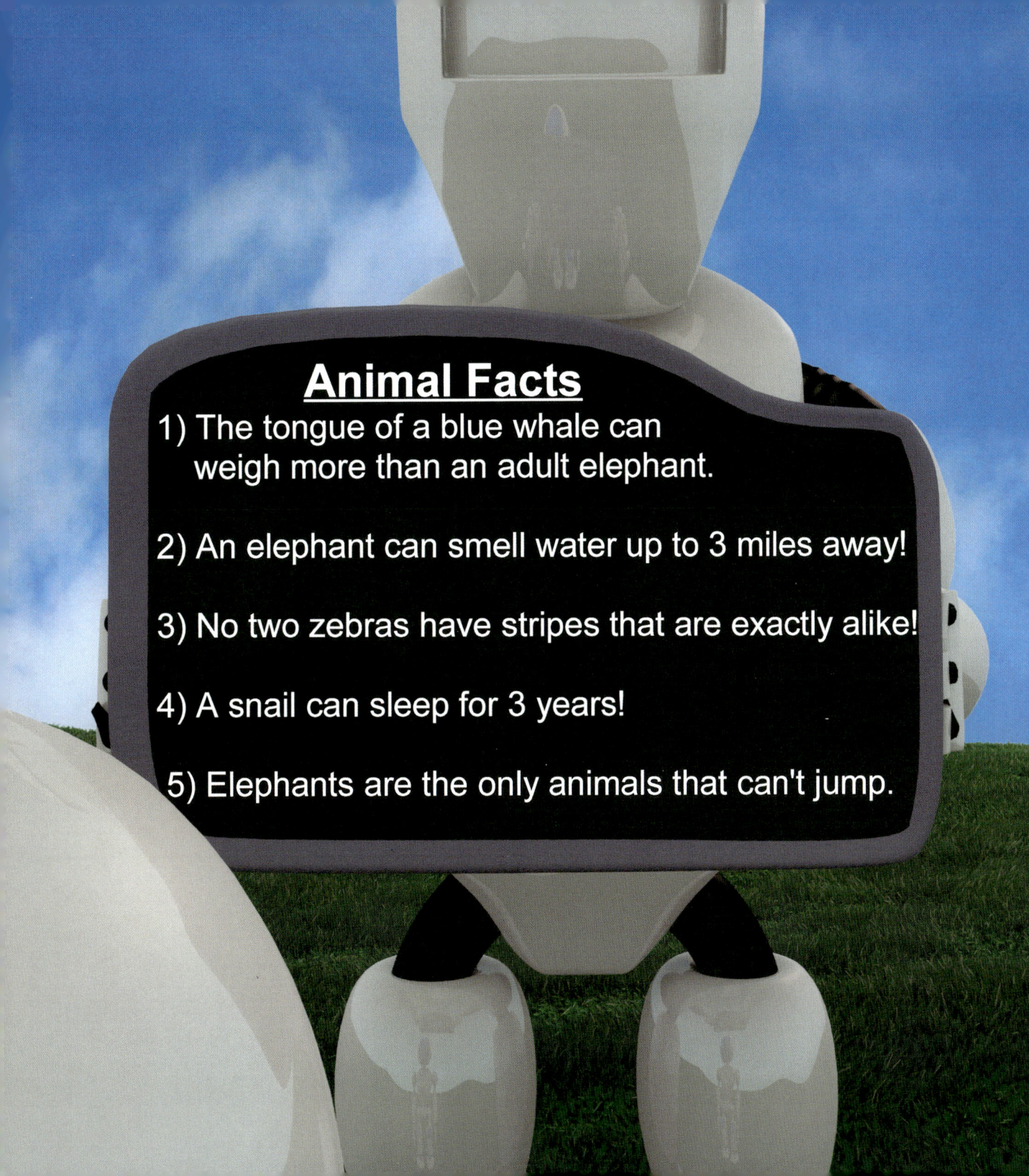

1) The tongue of a blue whale can weigh more than an adult elephant.

2) An elephant can smell water up to 3 miles away!

3) No two zebras have stripes that are exactly alike!

4) A snail can sleep for 3 years!

5) Elephants are the only animals that can't jump.

Glossary

Acacia Tree – A type of thorny tree or bush that grows in Africa.

Africa – A continent that is surrounded by the Mediterranean Sea, Indian Ocean, and the Atlantic Ocean.

India – A country in south Asia. It borders the Indian Ocean, the Bay of Bengal, and the Arabian Sea.

Mammal – A class of air-breathing vertebrate animals that have hair and three middle ear bones.

Zoo – A facility where animals are in enclosures and on display to the public.

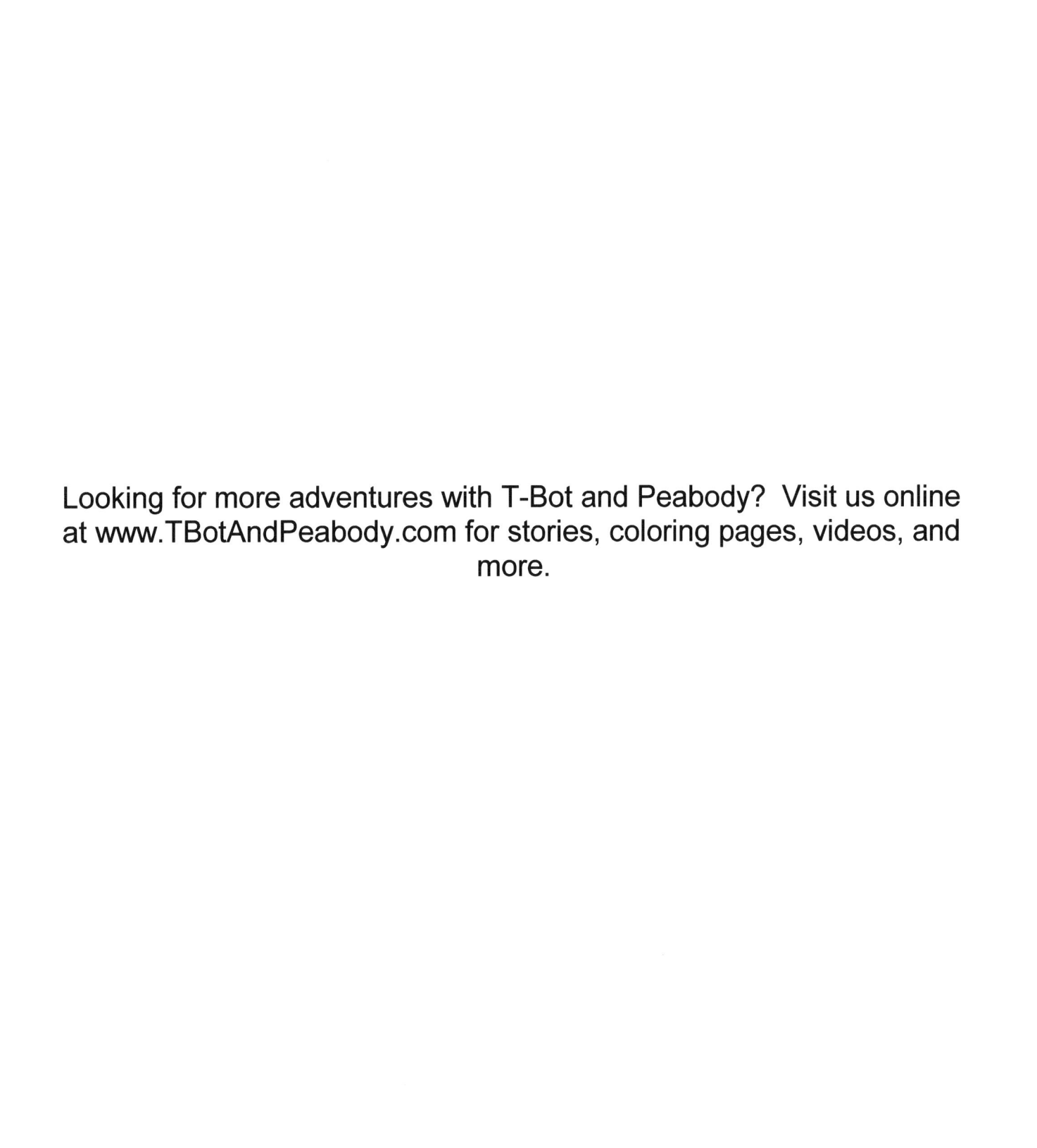

Looking for more adventures with T-Bot and Peabody? Visit us online at www.TBotAndPeabody.com for stories, coloring pages, videos, and more.

Special Thanks to our Photograph Contributors

Page 7
Black Rhinos in Ngorongoro Crater. Photograped by Mila Zinkova in Ngoro. c.c.3.0

Page 8
Bobosh T. via Wikimedia Commons

Page 9
Ursus Maritimus (Polar Bear) CC-BY-SA-3.0, via Wikimedia Commons
Ursus Malayanus by Sarefo CC-BY-SA-3.0, 2.5, 2.0, 1.0 via Wikimedia Commons
Bonobo at the San Diego Zoo. Photographed by Mike R. CC-BY-SA-2.5 via Flickr.com

Page 10
#2 by Steve Jurvetson via Flickr.com
#3 by Velo Steve via Flickr.com

Page 12
Giraffes photographed by Jon Ovington c.c.3.0 via Flickr.com

Page 13
#1 by hsivovev via everystockphoto.com
#2 by Chad Littlejohn via sxc.hu

Page 14
Caccamo c.c.3.0 via Flickr.com

Page 15
Caccamo c.c.3.0 via Flickr.com

Page 17
#3 by Stefanie Van Dervinden via photoxpress.com

Page 18
Manuel Gonzalez Olaechea via Wikimedia Commons

Made in the USA
San Bernardino, CA
02 October 2013